HOW TO BECOME A
PUBLICITY MAGNET
In Any Market via TV, Radio & Print

Havilah Malone

HOW TO BECOME A
PUBLICITY MAGNET
In Any Market via TV, Radio & Print

HAVILAH MALONE

5 STEPS TO WIN
In Your Personal & Professional Life

Be Seen. Be Heard.
Be Remembered.

Hemco | Publishing
Austin Texas USA

Havilah Malone

TO ALL THE DREAMERS OF THE WORLD

AND TO THOSE OF YOU WHO SUPPORT THEM

BECAUSE DREAMS *REALLY* DO COME TRUE!

.

Havilah Malone

Contents

HOW TO BECOME A
PUBLICITY MAGNET
In Any Market via TV, Radio & Print

Foreword

By Linell King, MD.

"Health is Your True Wealth." — Dr. Linell King

Who among us doesn't want to be known? Who among us doesn't want to be healthy? Who wouldn't want to help others to thrive and live better lives? The world is full of people who are suffering and need leaders like you and me to do whatever it takes to get our messages out there to help show them the way. If you are reading this book by Havilah Malone, then I have no doubt that you are also one of us who have stepped up to answer this calling within ourselves.

As a physician, I ran a successful hospitalist business helping patients through the entire process, from getting them into the hospital and providing their care, to getting them well enough to be discharged. I coordinated their entire post-care including facilitating specialists, getting them through rehab and ensuring that they had proper follow-up care with their primary care providers. I literally "quarterbacked" all of their care surrounding the hospital.

While I enjoyed what I did, I was not fulfilled. Not only was I seeing that patients could prevent being hospitalized if they would take better care of themselves, but also I didn't really have vitality in my own life. I was overweight and didn't have a lot of energy. Here I was, providing healthcare to others, yet I wasn't feeling healthy myself. So I decided to become a role model and take control over my life. I set new standards, transformed my health, and then set out to show others how to do the same.

I decided that I could use the same skills I utilized in the hospital and expand upon them outside of the hospital where I could reach more people and help them to prevent ever having to be admitted to the hospital in the first place.

That's what I did. Now what I do is help people by coordinating their journey to achieve ultimate vitality where they are not only free from illness, but also to where they can have an abundance of energy, achieve *and sustain* their ideal body weight and feel alive again.

Once you have decided that you are going to be a role model for others and utilize the media to get your message out, it's important that you *become* your own model if you want people to follow you. You will want to be your best self. You must be willing to transform every aspect of your own life in order to show the world not only your message, but also who you are as a person.

Unfortunately, many people keep their gifts locked inside of them or share what they know only with their friends and family, not realizing the value of their knowledge. They don't understand that others could benefit from what they know, but never do because their words are kept hidden. A lot of people think that they have to be perfect before getting into the public eye. But it's not true! All you really have to be is someone who strives for improvement and show that you are a survivor. Share your journey and let it be an inspiration to others.

What I admire in Havilah is that she noticed this inside of herself first, and then knew that she had to get her message out in order to help people like you and me do the same. You need a third party to help you to see the magnitude of your greatness because you are too close to yourself. It's hard to see the big picture if you are caught up in the frame. You need someone who can see your gifts and be able to pull them out of you. That is what Havilah specializes in doing. She has seen things inside of me that I could not see in myself. When I first talked to her, my vision became so clear, so simple. I thought, "Wow, why didn't' I see that?" That's her gift, to be able to pull that out of people. Then she guides you through the process of getting in front of the media in an authentic, effective way that attracts more media to you.

When I first met Havilah, I didn't know who she was or what she did. All I knew was that she glowed. She had an aura about her that lit up the room. She truly was a shining light. I could see people were drawn to her like a magnet. I didn't know why I wanted to be around her, I just knew I that I did. It felt good to be in the presence of her energy, enthusiasm and genuineness. Apparently, this was before she had decided to go down this path of helping people to find their greatness through the media, but she already had it in her. That was my first impression of Havilah.

As we became friends, I found out exactly what she did. It really made sense to me that she was in the public eye because she was, and is, so naturally captivating. She fully discovered that she had a gift to help people find what's inside of them, and in turn, helped me to find my gift within myself. With her guidance and intelligent support, I was able to reach far more people by amplifying my voice through the media. Subsequent to speaking on a radio show that Havilah coordinated, I've been invited to speak on other radio shows. More importantly, it strengthened my certainty that this is definitely the path for me to pursue.

Havilah pulled my radio show, *Ultimate Vitality Radio*, out of me. When she first mentioned it, I thought to myself, "Why would I have a radio show? I couldn't do that!" She encouraged me by telling me that I came across well, that I would be a natural at it and that it would be a perfect way to help get my voice and message out to the world. She then explained the process. Once she showed me the picture, I was able to see it and thought, "Absolutely I can do this!" That is how my radio show was born. I knew that not only would we have a great time creating it, but also this was something that was needed to help serve the health of others, which is my passion and purpose.

Through speaking, writing, personal coaching and strategic use of the media, I am able to reach a massive amount of people like you and help you take control over the direction of your life. I give you simple ways you can transform your health so that you can carry out your life's mission in a big way.

I encourage you to follow your purpose and passion, and then share yourself with others. It is important for you to do this. By helping yourself, you in turn help others. Start by becoming the best possible version of your true healthy self. Reach out and find mentors who can guide you. Become the mentor you want people to follow, full of life and vitality. And certainly utilize the skills of masters like Havilah Malone.

— *Linell King, M.D.*

Dr. King, author of **Simple & Sustainable Vitality,** is a speaker, educator, motivator and catalyst of change dedicated to helping others live exceptional lives with ultimate vitality.

www.DrKingEvents.com

Introduction

pub·lic·i·ty mag·net

noun (pə'blisətē magnət)

"Publicity Magnets are leaders, entrepreneurs and role models who easily attract media attention by adding massive value to others. They have a spirit to serve others and show up to win. As a result, they experience increased abundance in their personal and professional lives while genuinely helping to make our world a better place to live." — Havilah Malone

Hi, I'm Havilah Malone and welcome to the exciting world of *Publicity Magnet.* As you may know, when it comes to getting in front of the media, you only have one chance to make a great impression. In order to be successful, you must have a solid foundation within yourself along with knowledge and a strategic plan of action. That is what this book is about. In the following seven chapters, I am going to share with you valuable information that will help you to master your mind and emotions so that you can become attractive to the media and effectively get your message out to the world. Then, I will provide you with tips, insights and knowledge of the industry that will empower you to become the *Publicity Magnet* that you desire to be via TV, Radio & Print.

Just like you, I had to start somewhere. I had a dream to be on TV, but I had to take that first step which was to get *out of my own way*. I had to go from simply *wanting* it to happen to actually making it happen in order to be where I am today. My career as sought after spokeswoman, media expert and business strategist helping entrepreneurs, coaches, authors and leaders like you to become *Publicity Magnets* began as a production assistant at a local news station. From there, I worked my way up through broadcast media and gained experience in the industry by producing, directing, editing, acting, etc. I became well accomplished in front of the camera as well as behind the scenes.

It was through this journey that I discovered (and proactively found) concise actions that successful people took in order to get to where they wanted to be. I found mentors who exampled certain ways in which to think, feel, act, create and believe in order to be highly effective. Then, once I started implementing these techniques along with my experience in the industry, my career path opened up exponentially with far less effort. Endless opportunities began to appear. People in the media began to seek me out. I literally became a *Publicity Magnet.*

It's natural to make mistakes along the way but you certainly don't have to spend time or energy beating your head against closed doors. In the spirit of helping you to expand and achieve your success in the quickest, most effective way possible, I have summarized the secrets I learned for personal and professional success into **5 STEPS TO WIN** that I am about to share with you now. My intention is to help you overcome self-sabotage and limiting beliefs that are confining you so that you can truly create the life that you deserve. The fact that you are reading this book right now shows me that you are committed to taking the first step, and I want to commend you for that.

But, before we get started, let me ask you this: Do you ever wake up in the morning thinking that you might have a horrible day today? Do you worry that your day will be full of challenges and do you stress that nothing will get accomplished? Unfortunately, this is pretty common. This seems to happen some days... actually many days. And most people will experience overwhelming and concerning feelings that nothing is going right.

Sometimes it is so much easier to see where the pitfalls are in other people's lives and it's much more difficult to see them in our own. You might have identified a friend that you believe should change what they are doing so that they can live a happier life. But, you can't make someone else change. However, you can help by focusing your efforts inward and making shifts within yourself.

Let this book be a mirror for you so that you can create the life that you deserve. You are in a no-judgment zone and free to focus on what is here to serve you... and only you. Know that you are every bit as good and capable as anyone else you see on TV, Radio & Print. Whether you have allowed feelings of fear, low self worth - or simply just not knowing what to do stop you from taking that vital next step, this is an opportunity for you to give yourself permission now to grab hold of these tools and use them for *your own* success.

You will find concepts in this book that will really hit home with you. This is good. It is all part of helping you to remove blocks that are getting in your way. As this happens, take the time to pause and reflect. In order for change to happen, you must be willing to work through the feelings that come up for you. I will guide you through how to deal with these feelings so that you can step out in front of the public with confidence.

At the end of each chapter is an exercise designed especially for you to go even deeper. Whether you skim over them or expand upon them is completely up to you. You have full control over how much you want to invest in yourself. Handling disempowering emotions and investing in yourself is one of the best investments you can possibly make! Not only will you improve your life, but you will also improve the lives of others by showing up as a role model of strength.

Everything in this book is designed to help you get to where you want to be. There is nothing here that I, myself haven't experienced in one form or another. And I want you to know that I certainly did not do it on my own.

So sit back, relax, and enjoy your journey into the world of becoming a true, highly sought-after *Publicity Magnet.*

Chapter 1

M

I Came To Win!

*"Winners make habit of manufacturing their own
positive expectations in advance of the event!"*
— Brian Tracy

One of the things I really admire about children is their fearlessness. They will do things like jump off counters without hesitation or try weird foods without question. I remember once I took my niece and nephew to a sushi restaurant when they were just two years old. (They are twins and just the cutest little people I've ever seen!) I ordered cooked food for them along with a couple of sushi rolls for myself. When the food came to the table, they were both very curious about what I had on my plate.

My nephew, who seems to be the food connoisseur of the two, pointed at my food and asked, "What's that?"

I answered, "It's sushi."

Without missing a beat, he announced in his big two-year-old voice, "I like sushi."

I said, "You've never had sushi!"

He rebutted, "But I like sushi."

Who could argue with confidence like that? So I gave him a bite. He lit up and finished my meal by eating both my rolls!

That was a moment of realization for me. I began to wonder, "Where do our likes and dislikes come from? When did our fears and self-doubts creep in?" Kids have such an insatiable curiosity about their world. They will keep searching and trying different things until they find their answers. No matter how many times they fail or fall, they keep getting right back up again. They are not concerned about what others might think or say. They just play. What happened to those kids inside of us? Where do they go?

Somewhere along the line, while growing up, you start to lose sight of your inner child. You know, the one who believes that you are a superhero. You start to get buried under a mound of words like "No" or "You can't" or "You're not good enough." That invincible young dreamer turns into an overly cautious, self-aware doubter. Passion and purpose become trendy buzz words that are ever so illusive.

Although you may have attained monetary success or high status in life, there is still a place where uncertainty and self-doubt creep in and hold you back from living the true life that you desire. Does this scenario sound familiar to you? Well, I want you to know that you are not alone. Most people, including celebrities, superstars and those you see in the public eye have experienced this at one time or another. This was my story, too.

While growing up, I was a kid who was full of expression and I just knew that I would be on TV someday. I'd see myself talking to people, helping them out, collaborating with them and collectively changing the world. I saw it, I imagined it, and I dreamt about it. I was so full of life and unadulterated wonder. I would dance around my living room, singing at the top of my lungs and making dance moves that even *Dancing with the Stars* couldn't touch!

But as I got older, I started developing self-doubt as I began to learn the rules, regulations, expectations and limitations that others thought I should live by. I learned to act in the way I was expected to act. In other words, I started to live inside "the box."

Fortunately, my imagination would not be contained. One of my favorite movies when I was growing up was Walt Disney's 1989 animated film, *The Little Mermaid*. I especially related to Ariel (the little mermaid) when she sang "Part of Your World" and dreamed of venturing out of the world she was expected to be in and follow her heart into the world she dreamed of. In her story and in that song, I saw myself.

I was searching as to where I belonged. I didn't feel like the inside of me was congruent with the outside, and that caused the little kid inside of me to slowly shrink. I became so self-aware and worried about what others thought that I was always looking for the approval of other people. That followed me throughout my adult years. As a result, my self-worth became tied to my accomplishments.

I became addicted to high achievement as a way of proving my self-worth. I graduated from college when I was 19 years old, the same age when most people are just getting started. You can imagine that was a super exciting thrill for me at the time. Yet, the high of that achievement was short-lived as I started looking for the next accomplishment and the next fix to make me feel whole or worthy.

Right out of college I started my career in television by working for a local FOX station. Years later, I was lured into corporate America by the call of "job security" and I moved towards doing what was expected of me. I rose like a shooting star managing a 160 million dollar business. I worked with great people, held tremendous status in the company and reached high levels of achievement. However, I was not following my passion or fulfilling my dreams. Worse yet, I was not living up to my true potential, and I knew it.

I soon hit a threshold. I became miserable and stagnant. I felt like I was in a black hole of sorrow and darkness. I didn't feel worthy of the success I was experiencing. I found comfort in food, alcohol and so many other self-defeating behaviors. I certainly didn't want to disappoint anybody. I was always looking for approval from my family, friends, and peers. I never felt good enough. I would experience extreme highs, deep lows and then feelings of being alone. Have you ever felt like this?

Deep within, I wanted more out of life, but I had become afraid of change and failure. I feared what people would think if I weren't at the top of my game all the time, or if I didn't have a prestigious title tied to my name. I had traded in my dreams for a job (AKA, Just Over Burial).

Don't get me wrong; I *was* dabbling in my dream world. I made TV appearances, did public speaking and worked with charitable groups. But I wasn't fully living in it. I only had one toe in the water and held on tight to the so-called security of my job.

My mentor Tony Robbins says, "If you want to take the island, you have to burn the boat!" Well, I hadn't burned the boat or even set claim to the island. I was still floating out there 50 miles from shore looking through a telescope and waving really hard at the island of my dream-life. It was a painful experience. My real passion lies in helping people, yet I couldn't even help myself.

Then one day I got a message to jump on a conference call for work. That call was to inform our entire organization that our division was being dissolved and contracted to a third party company. We all had two weeks before being laid off. My world seemed to crumble in that moment as the rug was literally pulled out from under me. I felt confused, insecure and concerned about what people would think.

I faced a crossroad and had a very important decision to make. I could do what I thought others expected me to do, (i.e. find another J.O.B. which meant I would continue to die inside a little each day in the safety and comfort of so-called "security"), or I could step out into unchartered waters of the unknown, follow my dreams and answer the deep-down calling of that kid so full of life's passion and vigor. I could no longer ignore that screaming voice. I started to realize that *I* was the problem; nothing was going to change until *I* changed.

So I stepped out.

What I have since learned along the journey that followed has empowered me to where I am today. It is what I am about to share with you in hopes that you can bypass some of the mistakes I've made. My hope is to help accelerate you in living *your* life as you intend it to be lived so that you can move ahead and expand in your professional life as well.

THE BIG PROBLEM

So often, we are the blocks that get in our own way. It is that lack of self-confidence, feelings of fear or of low self-worth that can lead to three, really big problems: missed opportunities, addictions and regret.

Missed Opportunities - What would happen if you *did* go after that promotion... if you *did* try something new... if you *did* reach out to be a guest on that TV show... or if you *did* tell that person you have feelings for that you love him or her? At the end of the day, what would you have to lose, really?

When it comes to going after things you want in life, my initial philosophy is to realize that you presently are not in possession of that thing. If you decide to go after something and are denied, then you are no worse off than you were before you started because you didn't have it to begin with. So why hold back? Go for it! Go after those opportunities because missing them can leave such an empty hole inside of you.

Addictions - One of the most common addictions that you'll see (and you may have already experienced) is overeating (I.e. using food as a form of comfort to fill the void of where passion and action once lived). At one point in my life I suffered from being extremely overweight because I was constantly trying to fill that void with food. Alcohol is another means that people will use to numb the pain and subdue those empty feelings.

Regret - When you are not living the life that you know you are capable, then you are setting yourself up for a life of unfulfillment and regret. It is that sense of knowing what you want for yourself is passing you by. Living a life of regret eats away at your self-esteem and contributes to unfavorable emotions and moods.

I was in the parking lot of a shopping mall one day and I saw an elderly woman in a wheelchair, half slumped over and moving herself with a motorized knob. As I watched this frail, helpless woman slowly working her way towards an assisted living van, I couldn't help but be reminded of how precious life is.

Life is short. Don't waste one more day worrying about whether or not you're getting it right. Embrace this time you have before it's too late. Push yourself every day. Even do the scary stuff so that you never have to look back and regret what could have been.

Life is a gift and all we have is time. You can spend it being afraid of failure, worrying about what other people think and concerned whether or not you're good enough, or you can spend it creating and recognizing the opportunities in front of you. If you don't try, then you've already failed. If something doesn't work, then guess what? You just learned something! If that choice, decision or road you took didn't work out, then it just wasn't the right one to get you to your desired outcome. But in it was something for you to learn. It is these gifts of knowledge along your path that will help you to make different and better decisions next time.

Each and every one of us has been specially designed for a unique purpose. You can either step up to this journey called life to find and fulfill your purpose, or you can cower in your own shadows. The choice is really up to you. You are the *only* one who can stand in your way.

BE WILLING TO STEP OUT

So often people travel down the road of least resistance. They do that which comes easiest, but isn't always the best and usually is the thing that leaves them unfulfilled. It is easy to do the things that others expect you to do, and then blame them for things when they don't go right as opposed to taking responsibility. The only way to really be able to step into your full greatness and fully express the gift that you have been given is for you to try something new and step into the unknown.

This makes me think of the Wright Brothers, the inventors who are credited for building and flying the first airplane in 1903. Many people thought that they were absolutely crazy. At the time, who would want to fly through the air in a big metal box? Then I think about Alexander Graham Bell inventing the telephone, which led to us being able to talk to people all over the globe. At one time, that seemed insane. Yet it is because of people like them being unrealistic and stepping out to make their dreams happen that our lives are better today.

We are drawn to entertainers because they are willing to step out and do what most people are afraid to do. They wow us with their craziness and willingness to care not what we think of them, but what they can do to raise us up. They are willing to do the unthinkable, set unreasonable goals and live a life that most would claim is unrealistic. Secretly, we admire their courage and ability to step outside of their comfort zones and just be themselves.

> *"Being realistic is the most common path to mediocrity."*
> — Will Smith

The media is drawn to where people are drawn, and we are drawn to people who rejoice in the moment and radiate from within. Anybody can do this. All it takes is shifting your focus from caring about what people think of you to caring about what you think of people. How might you serve them? How can you share your gifts?

You have greatness within you and a gift that nobody else has. You were born to lead and get your message out to the world in a way that helps other people. I have written this book in an attempt to help you do just that. I will help you build your confidence and pitching skills so that you can use the media to magnify your message.

In the following chapters, I will give you five simple steps you can do now to help activate your mind and body in ways that will put you into the winner's circle. I've even created an acronym to make this easier for you to remember.

It looks like this:

5 STEPS TO WIN

1. **T - Think & Be Aware** - Facts vs. Fiction

2. **O - Open & Honest** - Be Truthful About What You REALLY Want

3. **W - Why Wait?** - Take Action NOW

4. **I - Inches Make Miles** - Measure & Track Results

5. **N - Now Celebrate Now!** - Celebrate each moment with an Attitude of Gratitude

I will give you clear direction and insights on how you can magnify your presence and become the *Publicity Magnet* you desire to be through TV, Radio & Print. Followed by that are resources that will help you to get started.

But before I do this, take a moment to do the following. Go back in your mind and imagine yourself as a child. Remember when you were in your zone, the play zone, when the world was yours and you could dream yourself into being what ever you wanted to be. Go there. Create the vision. Let yourself reconnect. Hear your laughter and feel the joy in your energy. See the future you saw for yourself. Relive being the king or queen of the world that you imagined around you. Reach out and solicit others to play with you, laugh with you and create together. Bring anything you can imagine into reality.

This, my friend, is the world that awaits you now.

Notes

What were your greatest memories as a child?

Notes

Havilah Malone

Chapter 2

Think & Be Aware

TO WIN

(Step I of 5 STEPS TO WIN)

"Everything that irritates us about others can lead us to an understanding of ourselves." — C.G. Jung

One day, I was minding my own business while driving down the middle lane of the highway. Suddenly, from the right-hand lane, a dark haired man (I'm guessing in his mid 40's) in a white four-door sedan cut right in front of me. I swerved and laid on my horn, but he just kept going. There was no courtesy wave or mouthing, "I'm sorry." Nothing! I got really aggravated. I just *knew* he saw me! I kept thinking what a jerk he was. My mind starting spinning with stories about how he cut me off on purpose. The madder I got the more my blood pressure rose. I started calling him some choice names (and not the ones his mother legally gave him!).

But now I look back on that situation and I really have to laugh. I can now see what really was fact as opposed to fiction. The story I told myself about why he had cut me off precipitated three to five minutes of me ranting and raving. Did that really work out for me?

THE TOTAL AWARNESS RULE

The Total Awareness Rule means that we have the ability to distinguish Facts vs. Fiction and we can apply this rule to every situation in our lives.

Let's take a look at the previously mentioned scenario and what I knew were the facts: A male in a white four-door sedan cut in front of my vehicle from the right-hand lane as I was driving down the highway. What other facts do we know that actually happened? He continued to drive up the road after cutting me off. That's about all the facts I know.

What our mind tends to do is fill the blanks where information is missing or unknown. We create what is known as fiction or stories, which are only theoretical or imaginary depictions of events. I assumed the man *knew* he cut me off. I could have been in his blind spot. I imagined him to be a jerk because he didn't acknowledge me when he drove in front of me. What if he had just gotten a call that his wife went into pre-mature labor and he needed to rush to the hospital? Do you think in that situation his mind would have been a little pre-occupied? Maybe he didn't even realize what he had done.

I'm not saying that's what happened, but isn't it funny how we immediately go to the negative when creating stories in our mind?

Let's also look at how I let the situation have an effect on me. I was aggravated. My blood pressure went up. I dwelled on the incident for three to five minutes. That level of stress literally takes time off of your life. Is any of this ringing a bell?

Is there any worth to creating stories that are not empowering? No! I have been cut off several times again while driving since that incident. Of course I don't enjoy it, but I have much better control over my thoughts and reactions because I immediately ask myself, **"What is fact? What is fiction?"** I then fill in the gaps with something positive like, "Oh, it was probably an accident or perhaps they had somewhere really important to go to and they didn't see me."

At the end of the day, it isn't about them. It's about the story you come up with. Deciphering the difference between what is fact and what is fiction is a tool you can use to make better more empowering choices for yourself. The voice in your own head is really the most important voice of all. If you are going to let that tape in your head loop and play the same message over and over again, then let it be the most empowering, inspiring and confidence boosting message ever told!

STOP, LISTEN AND LOOK

When you were in school during fire drills, do you remember being taught to stop, drop and roll? This was to condition you in an emergency situation so that you would know how to extinguish yourself in case you were on fire. Remember? Well, now it's time to **stop, listen and look!** Condition yourself in any given situation to take a look at the other person's point of view.

If you are not experiencing the kind of results you want in life, you're unhappy at work, your relationship is a mess, you're overweight and out of shape or you're feeling unfulfilled, trust me, you are in an emergency situation. The flames of the fire are burning high and it time to get those unwanted, unproductive voices out of your head. They aren't helping you. You must stop, listen and look at the results in your life to become aware of whether or not there is a problem. Then you can act appropriately.

WAKE UP!

You may have been on autopilot until this moment, making it through day by day as a reactive passenger in your own story. Well now's the time to wake up! Make today the day you take control of your life. Become the writer, director and producer of your own life. It's time to sit in the driver's seat, take control of the wheel and create the life you've always dreamed. This is *your* time. This is *your* season. You are good enough to do anything you desire and you have everything you need within you right now. Stop telling yourself stories that are holding you as a prisoner in your own body. If you have people around you that are tearing you down and telling you won't be able to accomplish your goals, then it's time to purge those voices from your head. It's time to wake up and become totally aware of what is fact vs. fiction.

Conditioning yourself to think and be aware is an important and useful tool that will become handy as you pitch yourself to the media. Rather than filling in the gaps with negative thoughts such as thinking that they don't want you, they're too full of themselves, or that they're jerks because they turned you down, you will get much further if you think and are aware of what is going on in their world. Put yourself in their position and try to see things from their point of view. I will I go deeper into this in Chapter 8 when I talk about understanding the media mind and becoming a *Publicity Magnet.*

You can sharpen this skill by taking the time now to think of a situation in your life where you may be filling in the gaps. What is really fact and what is fiction? What other possibilities could be happening that you don't see? How might you view this situation in a positive light? What can you think, do or say that will make you feel better about this situation? What can you think, do or say that would turn this situation into something that helps advance you towards your goals? If you hear yourself saying, "I don't know," simply put that aside and ask yourself, "What would it look like if I did know?"

Take all the time you need to explore this part of your life before moving on to the next chapter. Find ways to practice thinking and being aware of other people's point of view. Developing this skill will make life easier for you emotionally as you move forward into the public eye.

Notes

Fact vs. Fiction: What could have been the other person's point of view? How might I view past and present situations in a positive light?

Notes

Havilah Malone

Chapter 3

Open & Honest

T O   W I N

(Step 2 of 5 STEPS TO WIN)

"To believe in something, and not to live it,
is dishonest." — Mahatma Gandhi

In this chapter I will discuss how important it is to be open and honest about what you really want. The greatest lies that we tell are the ones that we tell ourselves. We hold ourselves back by dreaming too small.

Give yourself permission to really explore the possibilities of what you *really* want out of life. You must become crystal clear about what you want. You must be truly honest with yourself. That is an extremely important key.

OPEN TO POSSIBILITIES

I have a friend, Bridgeja' Baker, who owns a jewelry design business. She is a real go-getter in spite of the fact that she faced many challenges when she considered starting her own business. Many people told her she wouldn't succeed and that maybe she was being a little premature with starting a company. But she and her family decided to go forward with it anyway. It took a lot of courage to stand up for her dreams and goals and move forward towards them. She was open to the possibilities and followed her passion.

Now, she is doing extremely well and her business is growing by leaps and bounds. She has her jewelry on QVC, the world's top multimedia shopping company. In addition, she is to become one of the official junior jewelry designers for the first lady of the United States of America, Michelle Obama. What impresses me most about Bridgeja' is that she started her business in 2008 when she was only 10 years old! She is a remarkable young lady who truly shows that anything is possible.

So many times people stand in their own way with thoughts like, "I want to do this, but I'm too young," or "I want to try that, but I'm too old." If you look around, you will see that there is proof everywhere that anything is possible and that you can accomplish anything that you want. If you don't see the proof, then *be* the proof. *Create it!*

THE HONESTY RULE

I'm sure you've heard of the saying, "Know the truth and the truth will set you free." And my guess is that if you are like most people, it is not easy to hold to your truth in every given situation. Sometimes you may have a tendency to live in other people's world and be influenced by what other people think and say. You may have been influenced by others' opinions of what's right, what's wrong, or what should or shouldn't be a certain way. No worries. We've all been there rather than standing strong and taking action on what the truth is within ourselves. If you are one of the elite who stay the absolute course of honesty, then I commend you. If even in the smallest of ways you have waivered read on so that you can gain a broader perspective on the importance of how knowing the truth will not only set you free, but will also help you to intensify your magnetism, attract the media, and give you the ultimate ability to convey your true message to the world.

Have you ever been in a situation where, in the spirit of trying to fit in (or not hurt somebody's feelings) you went along with the crowd and pretended that you agreed with them even though inside you held a different truth? Well, you're not alone. Everyone has felt this disconnect at one time or another. But if you are not completely honest, then you dilute your ability to speak with authenticity and resonate with people on the level that engages them in a way that they trust you.

If you try to act one way when your inner thoughts are not in alignment, then your brain instantaneously sends mixed messages that your body reacts to. This incongruence expresses itself through a spontaneous body language that people pick up on both intellectually and subconsciously. I could list further scientific studies that support this (and encourage you to research it) but for now, what is critical for you to grasp is the importance of being openly honest with what you are thinking and feeling, even in the face of adversity.

The media jumps on topics of adversity! People who stand out in the media or who get quoted a lot are usually the people who are willing to speak their minds or who go against a popular opinion. People are attracted to someone who is willing to stand up for something that is bigger than them.

Look at Martin Luther King during the civil rights movement. He was willing to speak out on what people were thinking and feeling but afraid to say. He was open and honest with his own personal truth. He spoke honestly about what he knew deep down inside his soul needed to be said, even though it was obviously not the popular opinion. By doing this, he moved a nation! As a result, he became one of the greatest *Publicity Magnets* of all time.

People follow those who hold an inner peace of truth. People follow those who speak with honesty and authenticity. Don't worry whether people like you or not. The fact remains the more you worry about how much they like you, the less they are going to like you!

Regardless of what level you choose to play, know that it is okay to be different. It is okay to stand out. You are different. You are unique. That is what will propel you to the top! The more honest you are with yourself and others, the more freedom and liberation you are going to feel. Since you will no longer have an internal conflict, you will experience more peace.

You are more than the presence you project on an intellectual level. The essence of "You" happens on a molecular level. Everything that is genuinely going on inside your mind, body, heart and soul is what is being expressed on the outside, whether you know it or not. By being open and honest, you will align your mind, body, heart and soul and people will be able to feel it.

DREAM BIG!

The great American entrepreneur, author and speaker Jim Rohn said, "If you don't design your own life plan, chances are you'll fall into someone else's plan. And guess what they have planned for you? Not much." You can have anything you want, but it all starts with the way you think and what you believe is possible. It starts with you being open and honest with yourself. Then get clear and focused on making that desire a reality for you.

One of the most prolific contributors to the personal success movement was Napoleon Hill, who as a young writer, was given the assignment by Andrew Carnegie to go around the country and interview over 500 of the most successful people in the world. Some of those interviewed were Henry Ford, Thomas Edison, John D. Rockefeller, Theodore Roosevelt and many more. It took him nearly 20 years to complete this assignment. After making many discoveries, he summed up his findings in one of the greatest quotes of all time:

"If you can Conceive it, and Believe it, then you can Achieve it."
— Napoleon Hill

Now ask yourself, are you really dreaming big enough? Are you really going after what you truly want out of life?

Be open and honest with yourself about what you truly want and then DREAM BIG! When you start to think about your goals and aspirations, don't hold back. Dream HUGE! DREAM ENORMOUS!

Then write it down. This is an important step. There is something magical about taking that intangible thought from your head and moving it from pen to paper. Actually, a few things happen in that process. There is a neurological response of that thought moving through your body from your head to your arm and out through your fingertips to paper. It has been scientifically proven that you increase the likelihood of attainment of the things you want if you write them down as opposed to the ideas or goals you just keep in your head.

Another thing happening is that you are telling the universe that you are willing to take action. Think about it, if you won't even expend the energy needed to write something onto a piece of paper, how likely are you to follow through with any action that's needed to actually complete the task? It's not very likely.

So write it down. When we get to Step 4 of these 5, you'll really begin to see why.

Before you move on to the next chapter, take a moment to sit down and write out what you truly want for yourself. Don't hold back. Express what you want with emotion. Write with passion! To make it even more powerful, write with a sense of gratitude and a knowing that it is already waiting for you to claim as yours.

Then carry what you have written with you in your wallet or post it where you can see it everyday. This helps anchor you to that place of being open and honest with yourself, and having it readily available acts as a reminder to keep true to your desires and dreams.

Now start writing!

Notes

What do you REALLY want for your life?

Notes

Notes

Chapter 4

❦

Why Wait?

TO **WIN**

(Step 3 of **5 STEPS TO WIN**)

"Procrastination is the thief of time." — Charles Dickens

Let me ask you this. **What are you waiting for**? Now that you've decided what you really want and you know that there is no one stopping you but you, it's time to take action. NOW. There is no time like the present.

The average human life span is 28,782 days (approximately 78 years). When you break it down like that, it really helps you to appreciate that you don't have much time to waste. You must act now to accomplish your goals. If you think of each day as a dollar, then every day a dollar gets spent. Would you just throw it away? What value are you putting on that dollar?

Bronnie Ware, an Australian nurse who worked with dying patients during the last three to twelve weeks of their lives, found that there were some very common themes that kept appearing in her patients' conversations. She wrote a book called *The Top Five Regrets of the Dying*. What really struck me was the number one regret: "*I wish I had the courage to live a life true to myself, not the life others expected of me.*"

THE ALTMY LIST

Once time has passed and precious health is fading, people look back with so many regrets for the things they wished they had done. This fact struck me so deeply that it inspired me to get rid of my so-called Bucket List* and create and an Adding Life To My Years (ALTMY) list.

I know many people love the movie *The Bucket List* (starring Jack Nicholson and Morgan Freeman). In this movie, the two characters, who meet in a hospital while living out their last leg of life, set out to spend the end of their lives going on a world wide adventure to do all the things that they wanted to do before "kicking the bucket."

Although it really was a great movie, I didn't want a bucket list. I didn't want to wait until I was about to die to start living my life on my terms. I wanted to do so many of the things that would take my breath away. I wanted to add life to my years, so I created what I call an ALTMY List (I.e. Adding Life To My Years List).

A goal I always had was to run in a race. One day, I went to grab some lunch from a local sandwich shop and I saw a sign on the door about a 10K race that was coming up that weekend.

* A list of things to do before you die. Comes from the term "kicked the bucket".

My first thought was, "How cool would that be? I've always wanted to do that!" Then that voice of doubt crept in saying, "It's only two days away and people prepare months to do these races. I'm not ready. I'll do it someday."

But I always wanted to run a race! Then my mentor's words came to mind, "The quality of your life will depend on the amount of uncertainty you can be comfortable with." I took a stand for myself right then and there. I said to myself, "What am I waiting for? Screw someday! Today is the day!"

Now, I didn't even know how far a 10K was in miles, but I was sure hoping that it wasn't ten miles! Either way, I was committed to do it and have the experience. I needed to mark that item off my ALTMY List. So I went downtown the very next day and registered for the race.

On the morning of the race, there were thousands of participants lined up in their corrals. I heard the bang of the starting gun and began to move through the crowd to make my way along this 6-mile racecourse. At one point during the 2nd mile, I decided to actually run! At first I immediately wanted to stop and just walk. I had not been running in quite a long time, but I wanted to get the most out of this experience and I wanted to run.

I pushed myself to go further and further while all along fighting that voice in my head that begged me to slow down. But I found the harder I pushed myself, one step at a time, the further I could go. I had so many breakthroughs during that experience! I ended up running two miles in total. I was so proud of myself for taking the first step, which in reality was to take action, not to wait to live my dreams or do the things that I wanted to do.

TAKE IMMEDIATE AND MASSIVE ACTION

In the 2006 film *The Secret,* the Law of Attraction was popularized. Although I agree that our positive thoughts can create positive outcomes in our reality, thoughts are just thoughts unless we empower them by taking action. More specifically, you can sit around all day long imagining yourself on TV, but unless you get up and do something to make it happen, it's not going to happen! You must develop the skill to push yourself to step up and take action. That is where the magic happens. In the publicity game, opportunities arise all the time. Condition yourself to pounce quicker than others who are second-guessing themselves. This will place you in the forefront of the pack and the media will take notice of you.

Luck is where opportunity meets preparation. Make sure you are prepared. Being prepared will propel you for any opportunity to take action. Successful productivity is a result of preparation. The six P's for this are **Proper Prior Preparation Prevents Poor Performance.**

Just as an athlete conditions their muscles before an event, condition yourself by doing everything possible to be ready mentally, physically, emotionally and professionally. When you are prepared and willing to take immediate and massive action, you will then become heightened to see opportunities all around you. It's important to be prepared!

Today we live in an electronic world where people can look you up. As a result, it is imperative that your page or your bio is updated. Be certain that you have an online presence with a website or blog. Keep your Facebook page and/or social media up to date and interactive. Verify that you have your headshot, bio and testimonials ready for when opportunity presents itself. Make sure that they are an accurate representation of what you have to offer and true to your core beliefs.

I know this may seem like a lot to do. Do not get overwhelmed in making sure that all these pieces and parts are in place. The key is to start with one thing, do it well and then continue to build it one step at a time. You want to make sure that you are laying a proper foundation so that when the opportunity does arrive (and it will!) you are ready for it.

To better prepare yourself, work on clearing your fears as well. For example, if you have a fear of public speaking, you need to develop your ability to be an effective speaker, take time to practice speaking in front of a mirror or videotape yourself reading a book out loud. Or commit copy to memory and practice reciting. Practice expressing yourself emotionally and really feeling what it is you are saying. Invite family or friends to listen to you as you deliver some sort of verbal presentation to them. All of these will help you hone your skills and prepare you for speaking in public. The more you are prepared, the less fear you will experience.

SAY YES!

Be willing to say YES and try something new. Follow curiosities and explore new possibilities. You never know what doors are going to open for you or where opportunities might lead. This is the way I look at it; when you know what you want and where you are going in life, as opportunities present themselves, you will immediately get the answer to your questions from within your core being.

Sure, you may feel nervous and uncertain, but there's a difference in the feeling when that answer comes from truth rather than from a place of fear. That's what will help propel you to the next level. If that immediate, intuitive answer that comes to you is YES, then go for it. You are capable of anything and abundant resources are everywhere for everybody. Of course, this isn't about just saying YES to everything. It's about knowing your ultimate goal. When something comes up, tune into your truth, ask if this ties into your ultimate goal and if that first answer is YES, then say YES and figure it out. And you *will* figure it out.

Okay, you've got it! The next step is to go do it. What are you waiting for! Time stands still for no one. Take immediate and massive action on your goals right now. Ask yourself what is the one thing you can do right now, or in the next 24 hours, next week or in the next month that will help you get closer to what you want? What *can* you do towards getting that promotion, to getting started in your new business, to connect with a producer, or to get yourself more comfortable with speaking in public? Whatever your goal, what is the one thing you can do *right now?*

Get a pen and piece of paper and write down one thing that you desire most to accomplish in your lifetime. Act as if this thing is guaranteed to happen. Let your mind expand. Then, think of all the ways you can make this real. No holds barred! The bigger and broader you think, the more likely you will come up with ideas that excite you. Write down anything that comes to mind, big or small, simple or bizarre. Says YES to whatever those ideas are and keep it flowing, regardless of how outrageous or silly those ideas may seem. Circle something that you can take immediate and massive action on today (or within the next few days.) Do at least one thing every day until you are living that life you deserve.

Notes

What do you desire most? What can you say "YES!" to?

Notes

Notes

Havilah Malone

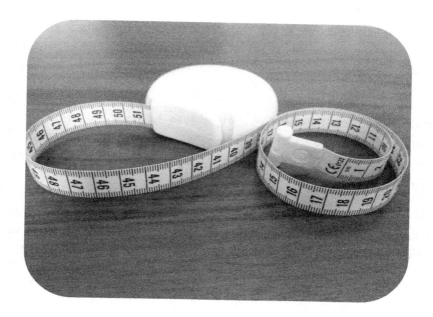

Chapter 5

M

Inches Make Miles

TO WIN

(Step 4 of 5 STEPS TO WIN)

"Life is a Journey, not a Destination." — Waldo Emerson

Now that you have your dreams well thought out, you are open and honest with what you really want and you are taking massive action to make it happen, the next step is to measure and track your results. How else do you know if you are getting closer to what you want?

Everything you do will either take you further away or closer to your goals. Every step counts. It is important that you keep track of what you are doing to ensure that you are heading in the right direction. As you measure and keep track of your steps, then going forward you will be able to adjust the action steps you take.

I have a friend who was on the air at a radio station that did not track their listeners. That station had no idea how many people they were reaching; let alone who their audience was (if any). They had difficulty getting advertisers because they couldn't say what their exposure was based on their listenership. My friend then moved to a radio station where they knew the demographics of their audience. As a result of measuring and tracking their listeners, they were able to determine the effectiveness of the show and in turn attract advertising dollars.

Simple tools I have found to be very effective to keep track of your progress are the Mark off Method and The 21-Day Account-ability Challenge.

MARK OFF METHOD

Because I stay very busy with traveling, speaking, coaching and filming, I tend to have several follow-up phone calls to make throughout the week. So I use the **Mark Off Method**. It is just as simple as it sounds. I have a dry erase board in my office that I write out a list of the people I need to call and the priority in which I need to call them. I move my way down the list, calling each one and erasing names until it's complete. It is very rewarding to take that eraser, remove a name from the list and to see the list shrink and shrink!

Use The Mark Off Method for anything you want to measure and track. A dry erase board is just one tool. If you have a smart phone, use your notes app. Spreadsheets work well, too. Heck, even sticky notes on the refrigerator! Be creative. It's important that you find what works for you and then do it.

21-DAY ACCOUNTABLILITY CHALLENGE

We all need support along our journey to help keep us accountable and encouraged so that we achieve our goals. A very fun and effective way to do this (not only for you but also for helping others) is by taking the **21-Day Accountability Challenge**. This is a great way to ensure that you get on track and stay on track.

Decide on a daily activity that you want to do on a regular basis that will help you to get closer to your goal. If you have a weight loss goal, then decide to do aerobic exercise for 30 minutes every day. If you have a sales goal for your business, decide to make a certain number of sales calls every day. Whatever that goal is for you, decide on one activity you can do daily that will serve you in reaching that goal.

Then, contact one or two close friends or colleagues and let them know that you are committed to doing this activity every day for 21 days. Ask them if they will be your accountability partners to ensure that you will keep to doing this activity every single day for 21 days. Find out what goals they want to reach, and then tell them you will do the same for them. You will want to select people who are just as committed to growth and making progress as you.

It is important to state your activity in simple, measureable terms. For example, "I commit to doing 25 push-ups every day before noon." Or, "I commit to practicing effective speaking for 30 minutes every day by 7pm." State the activity, quantity or duration and the time in which it will be completed.

Then start the challenge! After you've completed your daily activity, text your partners that you are done. It's that simple! As you receive the text from your accountability partners, send them a word of encouragement. They will do the same for you. Sending your text holds you accountable. Receiving the words of encouragement emotionalizes your accomplishment and helps to make this activity a positive experience. Of course, you are doing the same for your accountability partners, too.

Doing the same thing every day for 21 days is the approximate amount of time it takes to form a new habit. The reason most people don't stick to their goals is because they get off track and fall back into old patterns. When you are only accountable to yourself, it's easy to fall into the pattern of starting something new, falling off track then getting into that really low place where you feel disappointed in yourself. So then you get back at it, fall off track, feel bad and so on. Doing the 21-Day Challenge helps you break that pattern.

Now, let me make this real juicy for you. As human beings, we seem to have more stick-to-itiveness when we are being held accountable to someone else. So during the 21 days, if you or your accountability partners DO NOT complete your activity for the day, you all will have to start over back to day one. You certainly don't want to be the reason why the others have to begin again and vice versa. So execute the challenge and do whatever it takes to stay on track.

If you do mess up, be kind to yourself. Don't beat yourself up any more than you would beat up your accountability partner. Just laugh it off, get back up and do it again. Enjoy the process. Have fun along the way, day-by-day, one step at a time and do whatever it takes to get it done. The key is to keep moving forward. You'll get there! Remember, inches make miles of progress.

So what method are you going use to measure and track your results? What is one thing that you can do today to get you closer to reaching your goals? Who are you going to call to be your accountability partners?

442

Notes

What are your 21-Day Goals? Who will be your accountability partners?

Notes

Notes

Chapter 6

Now Celebrate Now!

T O W I **N**

(Step 5 of **5 STEPS TO WIN**)

"The more you praise and celebrate your life, the more there is in life to celebrate." — Oprah Winfrey

You did it! You took control of your life. You stopped making excuses and standing in your own way. How does that feel? You became very clear and honest about what you want. You are taking steps towards your goals and you are tracking your progress. Now it is time to celebrate! It's time to let that kid inside of you out to play.

Part of being a winner is making the time to celebrate. Not

stopping to do this is like a pilot being too busy flying the plane to stop for gas. Losers burn out and crash. Winners fly to greater heights by pacing themselves and celebrating along the way. Of course I encourage you to keep pushing forward towards your goals. But I also encourage you to interject the art of celebration as you are making progress, reaching milestones and achieving great heights.

THE IMPORTANCE OF CELEBRATION

Celebration is one of the most important, potent things you can do to make your life richer, fuller, happier, healthier and far more rewarding. It keeps you engaged in your purpose and helps you shine as the superstar that you are. Studies show that people who take the time to celebrate their successes along the way are far happier and healthier than those who don't. The simple act of celebrating releases hormones in your body that elevate your mood and improve your health.

By stopping to celebrate your successes (no matter how large or small), you magnify yourself as a happier, healthier, well-balanced leader who is *already* living a life of success. People will take notice of this. The more you celebrate, the more you generate the feelings of gratitude. The more gratitude you feel, the more you radiate as a positive person. The more you radiate as a positive person, the more you amplify yourself as being someone people will want to listen to. And, of course, the more you amplify yourself as someone people want to listen to, the more magnetic you become to the media.

So take the time to celebrate! Rejoice in your accomplishments *every day*. Do a happy dance the minute something good happens, even if you are only dancing in your head. This is for YOU. Your celebration can be as big or as small as you want and there are unlimited ways in which you can do this for yourself. The following is a list of ideas that I enjoy doing when I celebrate. Join in the fun!

10 WAYS TO CELEBRATE

1. Get a Massage - Nothing beats the relaxation and stress relief of a great massage, especially a foot massage. At minimum, take a few minutes to massage your own feet, hands, etc.

2. Tell a Friend - Call a friend and share your experience. When you share the victory with someone else, you reap the benefit of reliving the experience. You also pay it forward by passing along a little inspiration that moves that person into taking action on their goals.

3. Treat Yourself to a Luxury Item - Buy something for yourself that says congratulations! Maybe it's a car or a new watch you've always wanted. You can even have something engraved as a reminder of your accomplishment. Treat yourself!

4. Lose Track of Time - Spend a day doing whatever you want to do. Turn off your cell phone, shut down the computer, go for a walk, watch a movie or read a book. Do whatever your heart desires for the day; you deserve it!

5. Travel - Jump in the car, on an airplane or take a virtual staycation at home. Go to an exotic location like a Caribbean Island or skiing at a fancy ski resort. Get away with family and friends or go somewhere by yourself. Enjoy the break!

6. Pump up the Music - Dance! Sing! Move to the vibes! Play that air guitar while imagining an audience there just for you, screaming your name and celebrating your success.

7. Spend Time in Nature - Enjoy getting outdoors and reflecting on what you've accomplished and what great things lie ahead. Feel the wind on your face and the grass between your toes. Be in the presence of creation and let nature celebrate with you your contributions to the world.

8. **Laugh Out Loud** - Yes LOL! So often we suppress our natural feelings and expressions. To live fully we must express ourselves fully. So with each step, celebrate out loud! Laugh out loud! The joy of laughter is one of the best feelings you can ever experience.

9. **Look in the Mirror** - Look at yourself in the mirror like you are your best friend and thank YOU for getting yourself where you are today. Where there is gratitude, there is no room for negative emotion. The two cannot co-exist together. Gratitude breeds more success and more positive experiences. We always have something to be grateful for even if it's just that fact that we woke this morning and still have the gift of life.

10. **Pray** - Whether you believe in God, the Universe or whatever greater power that works for you, take a moment to pray. Say prayers of thanks and ask for continued guidance and blessings over your life. Pray that understanding, wisdom and faith will continue no matter what. Invite your Creator to celebrate with you and be a celebration in the lives of others.

Don't stop here! Think of different ways you can celebrate your accomplishments. Let your creativity and personality shine through. Find ways that genuinely make you happy and keep you inspired to keep moving forward.

What is something that you did today that you could celebrate? How might you celebrate it? How can you celebrate your simplest accomplishments? How can you celebrate your daily accomplishments? How can you celebrate your big wins? Who will you call to celebrate with you?

Notes

How might you celebrate your accomplishments?

Notes

Notes

Chapter 7

M

Fierce Faith

I CAME TO WIN!

(IMPLEMENTING the 5 STEPS TO WIN)

*"Ninety percent of what we fear never happens,
and of the ten percent that does, it is never as bad
as we feared it would be."* — Unknown

When we try to live within what feels normal or comfortable, we limit our opportunities for growth. It is human nature to avoid pain and take the path of least resistance. Yet the path of least resistance leads to mediocrity. It is also human nature to strive for improvement and growth. Therein lies the paradox. Lack of growth in itself creates a feeling of discomfort, which can lead to stagnation and pain. When pain outweighs the pleasure of comfort, you are then compelled to make changes and step out into the unknown.

It is the fear of the unknown that can be most crippling. In order to step into your purpose, your true greatness, you have to be willing to face change and experience something new. That can be very scary! Especially when you put yourself out there in front of the public.

It is natural to feel raw, uncertain and doubtful. You may experience emotions like fear, overwhelm, unworthiness, not being good enough or not being liked. You may be faced with indecision and moments of not knowing what to do. When you least expect it, feelings like these may surface when you strive to expand your horizons. Even the best of us who dream big, set unreasonable goals and forge ahead with ironclad determination are still as human as the next person and at times experience doubt. It's normal.

What makes us human is our innate ability to intelligently feel our own emotions. Quite often people will retreat when they are experiencing negative feelings. They will pull away from others and suffer alone. But if you try to figure things out on your own, you will set yourself up to spiral deeper into that emotional state that currently exists.

The thing to know is that you are not alone. These rotten feelings are natural. They have not come to take you down. They have come to pass, and it is through their passing that they will help you to stretch and grow. The greatest of leaders and most effective spokespersons understand this at the deepest levels. That is what makes them so magnetically compelling and believable. Once you face these fears and learn how to openly deal with them, you are then able to better connect with your audience because they will see that you understand them on this sacred level.

OVERCOMING REJECTION & SELF DOUBT

The great American actor, screenwriter and film director, Sylvester Stallone, wrote and starred in the Academy Award winning film *Rocky* (1976). He pitched his script with the intention of playing the leading role, however was rejected time and time again. He was then offered more money if he would sell the script and allow another actor to star in the film. Can you imagine? This was his baby, his idea, and they were telling him that he wasn't good enough to be in his own film. He persevered, turning down offers, until eventually a studio agreed to let him play the lead role.   Stallone says, " I take rejection as someone blowing a bugle in my ear to wake me up and get going, rather than retreat."

You are going to get rejected. It's the nature of the business. Your job is to *not* take it personal, but to see it as an opportunity to focus on what you can do to improve.

When I first started out as an actress, I auditioned for parts on television shows and movies. I would fully prepare, memorize the scripts, work all the angles, research the company and the casting director, etc. I would do a lot of prep work to ensure that I was on top of my game and ready to go. I would show up to the audition with confidence and come away thinking I had killed it I was so good. But then, I wouldn't get the call back. I'd be crushed! Doubt ran through my mind. I'd beat myself up wondering what I did wrong, thinking maybe they rejected me because of my weight, or because I didn't do this one thing or another. I came up with so many internalized excuses for why it didn't work out and I would be so worked up about it. But being in that state of mind only kept me from moving forward.

Fortunately, I began working with coaches and mentors who had been in the industry for years. They helped me to realize that rejections may have had nothing to do with me. Producers are looking for something very specific. You may be excellent at what you do, but not right for what they need. It doesn't mean that you didn't go in there and do a great job. It just means that you weren't exactly what they were looking for at that particular time. This is where applying the rule of **Think & Be Aware** (as discussed in Chapter Two) will certainly help you.

When you go after an opportunity and it turns out that you are rejected, understand that it wasn't the right opportunity for you. Take the lesson and keep moving on. Once-in-a-lifetime opportunities come along every few weeks so another one will be waiting for you. Most likely it will be bigger and better than the one that passed you by. Think of it this way, had you gotten the first one, it would have distracted you from the better one. Have faith. Fierce faith!

Remember, beauty is in the eye of the beholder! If you fear that you are overweight, remember the only size that truly matters is size healthy. Societies' image of what is large or small and what is pretty or not continually changes like the shifts of the wind. Set your own standard. If there's something you don't like, then change it. Be who you are and own it. It's okay to be, do or have anything you want, especially when that burning desire comes from a place of love. When you love and appreciate yourself enough to want the best for yourself, then you'll win every time. And you came to win, right?

IF YOU CAN'T THEN YOU MUST

Although I always tried to put forth a strong front, I have certainly had my moments of weakness. What I most feared was putting myself out on the line. I never wanted people to see me being vulnerable or to think that I couldn't handle things. When I was building my business, I reached a time when I needed help, yet I was too proud to reach out. It finally got to the point where I became nearly frozen in my own tracks. Sure, I could function and go through the motions, but I suffered this pang of incongruity by putting on a happy face yet harboring those feelings of fear inside my soul. I needed help. I was afraid if people saw me being less than perfect then they would view me as weak. Yet, I couldn't shake those feelings myself.

I had to face my own internal fears. I knew the power of the statement *If You Can't Then You Must* and had no problem applying it when it came to my business or adventurous endeavors. In fact, I prided myself in being able to take action whenever something scary came up in those arenas. Time and time again I would face a fear and say to myself, "If I can't then I must!" and then I would just go for it. I would literally feel the fear and do it anyway. And every time, the rewards on the other end were worth it. Yet this was different. This was an entirely deeper level of uncertainty. This was dealing with my greatest fears in the depth of my soul. This was facing my nemesis, which was my fear of others seeing me as weak.

The more I tried to handle it myself, the worse those feelings became, until one night I fell into a funk. The words "Ask and you shall receive" played over and over in my mind. Ask and you shall receive and if you can't then you must. That is when the lights went on and the rubber hit the road. I knew something had to change, and that change was _me_. So I took in a deep breath of fierce faith and made my move.

I decided to post my fears and vulnerabilities to a private Facebook group and ask my confidants for help. I poured my heart out. Then, wiping the tears from my eyes as they dripped onto the keyboard, I pushed the send button. Instantly, a rush of doubt rippled throughout my body. "Are you crazy?" I thought to myself. "What the hell did I just do? What is everybody going to think?"

Within moments my anxiety turned into awe as an outpouring of massive love and support came back to me in a wave of posts, texts and phone calls. It was beyond anything I could have imagined. People told me that they too felt the same way at times and shared what they did to break through. It was like receiving the golden pass to come inside and see that we are all going through the same struggles. I came to understand that showing my vulnerability is not being weak. I wasn't crazy. And I most certainly wasn't alone.

IMPLEMENTING THE 5 STEPS TO WIN

It's one thing to understand this in theory, but you won't fully understand it until you experience it. That is why faith is needed. I can tell you about it all day long, but when you go through it yourself, it becomes real for you. What is important is for you not to block your growth and progress. Hold the faith that everything needed is inside you to get you where you want to be. You have the right tools. Use those tools.

Step 1 of the **5 STEPS TO WIN** is to **Think and Be Aware**. When you are in those times of despair, know that you are not in a position to be thinking clearly. Your body has become flooded with hormones that create the emotions you are feeling, and the more you think about those feelings, the more those hormones get released. Simply be aware of this, and then break the pattern. The quickest way is to change your state by reaching out to your support group. Be smart and avoid anybody who is going to participate in your pity party! Connect with people who give you empathy (not sympathy), who support your vision and help you get back on track.

Step 2 is to be **Open & Honest**. Don't hide. Get clarity by being totally open and honest with yourself, and then be willing to show your true self to others. Nobody likes a person who is always one note or lacking in emotional range. Allow those feelings to surface. Be fully expressive. This will be evident in your presentation, the delivery of your information and in your confidence on camera. People will be able to really feel you. The more you face your fears and get real with yourself, the more people will pick up on that and be attracted to you.

Step 3 is **Why Wait?** If you are unable to change your own state, reach out to the people you trust who will have your best interest at heart. Be real and authentic with them. Give them the honor of seeing you for who you really are, the good and bad, the pretty and the ugly. By doing so they will only love and respect you more. You are not alone, and you will notice that as soon as you learn to open up.

Obviously, you don't want to hold people captive by wallowing in your story. That is not the winners' way. Sure, you may get a lot of attention at first, but it won't be long before they tire of you and you lose their support. It's okay to share your story and feel the pain, but it's not okay to live there. The idea is to acknowledge your feelings, reach out, accept the help and get back to fulfilling your purpose as soon as possible.

Step 4 is **Inches Make Miles**. Not every step you take will seem like it is getting you to where you what to be, but indirectly it is, so keep moving forward. Unlimited opportunities and potentials are available to you if you just step into faith. I love the scene in the 1989 film *The Last Crusade*, where Indiana Jones (starring Harrison Ford) has to get to the other side of an abyss. He must trust the voice of his father that he hears telling him that he must believe. As Indy holds his heart, and as he takes his first step, the bridge magically appears beneath this foot. He had to take that leap of faith and take the first step.

When you are willing to put yourself out there and take that step, either the next step will be waiting for you like it was for Indiana Jones, or you are going to learn how to fly. What if you did go after something and it didn't work out and you fell flat on your face? Well, you know what? That was not a failure! That is not a step backwards. That was an opportunity to learn something. Now you know that didn't work and you can try something else.

Anytime you feel stuck, frustrated, confused or fearful, lean into it. You are about to have a break through. Night is followed by day. Tension is followed by release. And frustration is followed by a break through. Reach out and move forward. Each break through makes you stronger. After you go through times like these with your friends, be sure to celebrate with them as you learned in **Step 5** and that is to **Now Celebrate Now!** You just had a break through!

WINNERS RITUAL

Some people accomplish great heights while others seem to never have enough time to get anything done. Yet, we all have the same amount of hours in a day to do the things we want to do. If you want to be a winner, then look at what the winners do. One of the things most winners have in common is that they practice daily rituals that propel them towards their goals.

What you do today determines what you are tomorrow. You probably have the ritual of brushing your teeth every morning and every night to keep your teeth clean and healthy as well as to prevent tooth decay. Now, add to that routine the empowering actions that will energize your body and condition your mind to bring out the winner you desire to be.

Following are examples of things you can do. You will certainly want to be creative and do things that you find fun and enjoyable so that you will do this everyday. If you are thinking that you don't have the time, then do this while you are in the shower or driving your car. There is always time. By creating a Winners Ritual for yourself and making it a priority, you will become that winner.

Breathing - Your body needs oxygen more than it needs food or water. By giving your body the oxygen it needs, you will immediately feel energized. Make it a habit of breathing deeply everyday. Take a deep breath into your belly, hold it, and then slowly let it out. Repeat this at least seven times and try to do it three times during the day. Your body will thank you for it. This will also become a great habit to help you subdue those nervous feelings you may have of being on camera.

Visualization - As you are breathing deeply, imagine yourself already being that superstar you seek to be. Your mind doesn't know the difference between what is real and what you are imagining. By visualizing, you are tricking your brain to believe that you already are what you have imagined. That is why it is important to hold positive thoughts as much as possible.

Power Walking - Where the mind goes, the body follows. So be aware of how you hold your body. A powerful routine is to get out and power walk (or if you are a runner, get out and run). Hold your head high. Breathe deeply, imagine that you are a winner; walk with purpose. Not only is power walking great exercise for you, but also it physiologically helps you to clear your head. With every step you take, know that you are walking into your destiny.

Incantations - Power up your power walk with incantations (i.e. a series of statements that reinforce your vision). Say them out loud and empower them with emotion. Following are some of the incantations I like to say. You are welcome to add them to yours:

- Every day in every way I fully embody my God-given gifts and talents.
- I easily and frequently attract media attention so that I can serve others by sharing my message with the world.
- I am proof of what's possible.
- I am a Publicity Magnet.

Bookend Your Day - Winners take control of their thoughts and direct them as they choose. We bookend our day by thinking empowering thoughts first thing when we wake up and last thing when we go to bed. Your brain is your servant. Give it the job to serve you in a positive way so that you experience positive outcomes throughout your day. When you first wake up, take immediate control of your mind. For example, by telling your brain that the solution you seek is already found and that opportunity is everywhere and is seeking you out, you are then calibrating your mind to be in tune with opportunity when it presents itself. Basically, what you are doing is setting the television set in your mind to the right channel. This way you are allowing great opportunities and abundance to flow into your life rather than blocking them by being subject to whatever is going on around you.

A Winners Ritual is intended to condition you for a mindset of win-win. By helping yourself, you can in turn help others. By magnifying your own talents, skills and attitude, you can then become a greater resource. Wanting to make the world a better place is certainly noble, but it starts with you in your own camp and in your own mind. You need to take the time to make your own soul the better place first. By taking care of yourself, you will be more fulfilled and live a happier and healthier life. More money is going to flow to you. More people will take notice.

Reinforce yourself every day by creating a Winners Ritual and implementing the 5 STEPS TO WIN.

Havilah Malone

Notes

What will you do everyday to condition yourself to win?

Notes

Notes

Chapter 8

M

Become a Publicity Magnet

I CAME TO WIN!

(<u>ACTIVATING</u> the **5 STEPS TO WIN**)

*"Whosoever will be chief among you, let him
be your servant."* — King James Bible

At the end of the day, it's about asking yourself how you can best serve the other person. Build your messaging around what people need, not what you want, or what you think they need. In other words, what powerfully attracts the media, as well as the public, is when you make it about them, not you. You will find the media knocking down your door (so to speak) once they discover that you have something to offer and you are offering it in a way that serves the needs of their show as well as their audience. It is through the spirit of giving back and serving others that you can create a timeless legacy for yourself. You win in so many ways, but first, you must get out of your own way and seek to serve.

FREE PUBLICITY

Not only am I sharing with you how to be a publicity magnet so that the media seeks you out, but I am also sharing with you that it can be done without having to pay your way in. Most people think being on TV is elusive. Well, I am here to tell you that it isn't. You can do it for free. That's right, for free!

Publicity is far more powerful than advertising. You can reach more people, attract more business and make a greater impact with your message, all without having to pay. You can spend a fortune in advertising dollars trying to accomplish this, but why spend all that money on advertising when publicity is free?

Did you know that when a producer calls you to be a guest on their show, you don't have to pay? There are some radio shows where you can pay to be a guest, and this is certainly a good way for you to get started. But when you understand how the media works, you can easily get them to take notice and come after you.

Media builds upon media and the more you are in the media, the more the media will want you. I had built up a strong online presence, and as a result, I was asked to be a guest on a radio show that normally charges their guest. Because they approached me, I didn't have to pay. The interview went really well.

As soon as I got off the air, I had a message through Twitter from a woman who hosted another radio show. She had caught the end of our interview, liked what she heard and was interested in interviewing me for her show. Some shows will even pay you, but you have to be a *Publicity Magnet* to attract that. If you apply the principles in this book, you will certainly be well on your way to being paid for your appearances.

Being a *Publicity Magnet* through TV, Radio & Print brings your business to an entirely different level as you differentiate yourself from your competition. When you see someone on TV, or hear him or her on the radio, you automatically assume that person to be an expert, right? The general public will pay more money to experts for their products and services than they will to the typical person in business. For example, if you see a résumé writer as a guest on a local TV show and they are talking about the top five things you don't want to do in a job interview. Well guess what? When you go to have your résumé written, are you going to call just anybody or are you more likely to call that expert you saw on TV? Yeah! You're going to call that expert, because in your mind, that person *is* an expert since you saw them on TV!

WHERE TO START

It is extremely important for you to have an online presence. I can't emphasize this enough. That's where the producers are going to look once they hear about you. They will look for your website and check you out to see how you will appear on their show. The following are definite things they will look for:

- **Bio Page** - Start with what you are currently doing, your recent accomplishments, and build backwards from there, unless there is something highly significant in your past. You will certainly want to list that up front.

- **Video** - Have a website with video content that shows you demonstrating your product or service, or perhaps talking about your book. Experiential selling is very effective and this shows producers your ability to be interactive on their show. So the more clips showing you doing this, the more alive and experiential you can make it, the better it will be for those seeking you out. Visually, make it powerful by

83

showing the process of going from here to there. Show before and after results (i.e. if you do this, then that will happen). Show them rather than telling them. People love the visual experience.

- **Testimonials** - Gather testimonials from people with whom you have worked and add those to your website. Ask people to post something on your Facebook page about how great your product or service is, what a privilege it was to work with you or how you helped them in some way. People look for social proof. Have testimonials that grab their attention and leave them wanting to know more.

Producers are out there constantly searching for people and new material. It's their job to find really interesting stories of people they can present as experts. They look for great guests who will fit their target audience and have a message or information that is going to benefit them. You have to understand what they need and how you can fulfill that need with your product or service, not the other way around. It's not about going in with the thought that you need to be selling something. Don't worry about that. The publicity itself is going to help skyrocket your business.

When you get quoted in any kind of media, it will be of benefit to you because that will go down in history as an addition to your credibility and proof of your expertise. When you have the opportunity to get quoted, or interviewed via TV, Radio & Print, you can then take those media appearances and add them to your portfolio as well as your online presence. If you are a doctor and you were quoted in an article, you can frame that article in your office. This type of social proof will build additional confidence in your patients as they see you as a subject matter expert in your field.

As you do interviews, add those clips to your website and then link them to other media outlets. Once you are featured in the media, more media will want you. Being featured on a show and being able to add that to your website will add so much more credibility and differentiation and, as mentioned above, will give you an expert status that you couldn't buy.

UNDERSTAND THE MEDIA MIND

It's important to understand the media and then figure out where you can fit in by being of service. Remember? It's not about you. It's about what value you can add to them. The best way to start learning about how the media works is to watch and listen to as many shows as you can that are in line with your message. You must know which show is right for your product or service. Pay attention to which audience and which show segments fits what you are offering. If you are pitching a very light topic to a hardcore news station, they are likely to think you don't know their show or their audience. Align yourself to the show format that best fits you, as you would align yourself to the best career that fits you. You then become a better fit for each other.

There are industry specific shows. If you are in the medical field, look for medical shows like *Dr. Oz* or *The Doctors*. I would definitely recommend you start off with building your brand in your local market. You can approach your local affiliate stations. Most of them have a four-hour morning show and they need to fill that time with content. They are constantly looking for guests. This is a great place to start. But before you approach them, be sure to watch their shows and pay attention to the type of stories and topics that are shown in the program. If one of the anchors or reporters does a lot of human-interest stories, or there is a segment in the news about health, find out who the producer is of that segment. That is the person you are going to be sending your pitch to.

Understanding what their show is about, what their segments

are and how can you fit into that picture and add value to their audience is all a part of understanding the media mind.

Then, it's all in the way that you approach them. If you approach them saying, "I have this new product out and we just wanted to blah, blah, blah..." then they will simply direct you to their advertising department. But when you approach them with a catchy, attention-grabbing story that is going to serve their audience, they will want to talk with you and see what you have to offer. You have to approach them with the mindset of serving them by being a resource to them and their audience.

Have an understanding of who is who in a station based on the type of station you approach. For example, to get past the news station door, you'll want to know the receptionist. He or she is basically the gatekeeper. The production assistant is in an entry level position that helps out doing all the task work such as printing scripts, filtering calls, etc. Then you have the producers, assignment editors, reporters and anchors. Additionally there are people throughout different departments such as production with camera operators and directors. The station manager oversees them all.

Unless you have a direct line to someone, when you call in you are going to get the station's receptionist. You certainly want to acknowledge that person and keep him or her happy. (Keep in mind that you are dealing with people first, then the position they are in. Treat people the way you want to be treated and show your appreciation. A little kindness goes a long way.) If you have an interview and you need to show up in person, you will also meet the production assistant who will escort you to the producer. The producer is the one responsible for the formulation and success of the show.

Getting into print is very similar to getting on TV or Radio. You need to understand the publication that you are reaching out to. Get to know who the writer's are. Make note of their style.

Follow their work and read their articles. Look for trends in what they are writing about most. Then, before you reach out to them, you can construct a statement (or hook) that will be of interest and catch their attention. Keep in mind that they are motivated to fill ad space. They may want you to take out an ad first to build a relationship with them before they do a story on you.

BUILDING RELATIONSHIPS

Take the time to build genuine relationships and make friends with everybody you can in the media, not just the producers and hosts. Everybody starts somewhere and you never know where he or she is going to end up. For example, when I started with the news station, I used to be a production assistant and the young lady who was one notch above me went on to become an anchor on one of the local news stations. I went on to become a national spokesperson and television host. So you never know. Treat everyone with equal respect, regardless of his or her position.

Do what you can to be of service. Be kind, sincere and present. Obviously, you never want to be fake or pretentious. They will see right through that. However, if you are inclined to bring doughnuts, then do so. More than just cops like doughnuts!

You will especially want to get to know the producers and become an invaluable resource for them. It is important that you always efficiently and effectively follow up. Take the time and get to know them on a personal basis. Care about who they are in both their professional and their personal lives. Find out what they need, and then deliver it to them to make their job easier. If you are invited to do an interview, provide them with a list of questions they can ask you. Anything you can do that is helpful will put you in the forefront of their minds. You will evoke the law of reciprocity and they will want to help you out as well, as long as you are genuine, dependable and provide them with what they need.

It's pretty simple really. Be fully who you are. Allow others to fully be who they are. Then interact in a way to be able to add value to each other. This way everybody will get what they need.

THE PITCH

You are ready to pitch yourself to a station once you understand what the show is about, what they need, how you can benefit them and you are clear that what you have to offer is applicable to their audience. The best time to send in your pitch, preferably via email, is Tuesday through Thursday between 8:30 a.m. and noon (Central).

The structure of a pitch is pretty simple. Start with who you are, what it is you do and how you can benefit their show with what you have to offer. Attach a press release if you have one. Remember you are not selling to them, you are offering them a solution to their needs. In the subject line, write a hook that catches their attention.

Make your hook creative, catchy and interesting. It needs to be one that they will be able to share with their audience. Solve a problem for them. Examples of catchy hooks would be *Top Five Ways to Stop Procrastinating and Start Living Big* or *How To Make Money While Your Kids are At School Even if You Don't Have a Computer.*

On the slow news days, producers will be looking for content to plug in. If you have prepared yourself, been reaching out, sending out press releases and building relationships, they will call you and plug you in. You will become their go-to person on a regular basis whenever they need an expert guest.

OPPORTUNITIES EVERYWHERE

Know what's going on in the media in general. Know what is on top of people's minds. What are the hot topics? What are the needs and concerns? Tie your message into what is currently going on with people, society, the world, etc. This broadens your opportunity to speak on several different topics.

A great exercise for this is to look through magazines or newspapers and see what the headlines are. Then craft your expertise and message around what the current needs and concerns are. The more you do this the more you will be spontaneously ready to speak on any topic. An example of this would be when there was a lot of interest in Kate Middleton, Duchess of Cambridge and wife of Prince William, when she was pregnant with the royal baby. If you are an accountant, you can talk about financially preparing for a baby. If you are a health coach, you can talk about proper diet or exercise for a pregnant mother. You can even use the name of the celebrity in your hook.

The more you practice and sharpen your skills, the more you'll be able to identify and jump upon opportunities when they arise.

There are industry publications where reporters will put out a topic or questions for a story that they are writing. This is done to encourage comments back from experts in the field. If you reach out to them and are able to provide the information they need, you may be quoted in their article. Many times this gets picked up nationally.

These are just a few ideas but there is so much more. There are opportunities out there around you everywhere in every form. We can certainly help guide you.

FORMING ALLIES

For instance, what if you see a reporter who continually interjects herself into her reports, talking about how her mother overcame breast cancer? Perhaps she has an affinity for breast cancer awareness or organizations that support a cure. You can then specifically pitch to or approach that reporter about a breast cancer awareness initiative that you have going on with your organization and invite her to come be a speaker. Making her your advocate and bringing her on board with something you are doing brings your two worlds together.

SHOWTIME!

You *never* know when opportunities are going to come your way. It's important in the mornings that you get up, dress up and be ready to go. Even if you are doing a radio interview by calling in from home, dressing up will help put you in a state of feeling good and keep you on top of your game. The majority of the radio interviews I do are via Skype or my cell phone because that's the way technology works these days. But I don't just roll out of bed and do these interviews in my pajamas because I would be in a different state of mind. Actually, while I'm doing the interview, I am up walking around and getting into the flow of things. More energy comes through and I am able to better express myself over the phone.

Another thing to keep in mind is that TV shows may call you first thing in the morning because they have availability and need you to fill the slot. When you get the opportunity you want to make sure you can roll with it, jump on it, show up and do the best interview possible.

In preparation for being on camera, or a radio interview, you do want to make sure that you are prepped physically, mentally and emotionally to have that conversation. Take care of your health. Be well rested. For interviews that you will be doing face-to-face, avoid wearing perfumes, smoking or eating smelly foods like garlic. I'm serious. You don't want to stink!

Always show up on time. Need I say more?

When you show up at a television station, there will be someone to greet and escort you to the studio, green room, or wherever it is they need you to go. You will more than likely meet the producer and have a conversation with him or her as to what the plan is. Usually there is a sense of urgency on set and in the station because they are producing what is more than likely a live show and there are a lot of moving parts in production. Make sure that you are not getting in the way and are tuned into what is going on around you.

Learn to speak in sound bytes. Sound bytes are short and to-the-point statements that allow a conversation to be a pitch and catch. A typical interview on a TV show may range between five to seven minutes or longer depending on the type of show it is. But whatever your time frame is, you want to speak in a way that is memorable, to the point and quotable. Then, when they are advertising the show afterwards through social media or advertising, you may very well be quoted from something you said in the show.

When people are nervous, they have a tendency to talk too much. But if you are long winded and totally dominate the conversation, you will become repelling to the audience. Not only are you more than likely not going to be invited back, but also others will not want you on their shows either. This is why it is important that you spend time preparing yourself, practicing and recording yourself on camera.

Learn to be a very good listener. If you are acutely, actively listening to what the host is saying, then you won't be so much in your head. You won't miss anything. They may make a good point that you can play off of and take the conversation in a really great direction, but if you are in your head it may be missed. Be present and stay present.

Another great skill to possess is being a really good storyteller. We are a society that understands things through stories. The better storyteller you are, the better your message will be received. Combining the art of storytelling with the skill of being an active listener creates a comfortable flow that will captivate your audience and leave them begging for more.

Not long ago, I went to pick up some food from a little café in a shopping center near where I live. As I was coming out of the restaurant with food in hand, I saw a reporter with a cameraman doing some filming. Of course, I was curious. The reporter approached me and asked me if I lived in the area. I said, "Yes" and we started talking. She told me that they were doing a story on how to attract more professionals to the area and asked me if I would be interested in doing an interview for the news broadcast. I said, "Sure!"

Be on the lookout for opportunities wherever you are. You always want to be ready, willing and able in any given moment to go on camera. When you fully embody the **5 STEPS TO WIN** and live in the space of seeing your self as a *Publicity Magnet*, your mere presence will draw media to you.

When you see news vans or reporters on the street, definitely approach them and strike up a conversation. You never know what they are looking for and chances are you may be the solution to what they need. Approach them with the intent to serve. You may be exactly what they need or you may have a resource to which you can connect them. Don't let opportunities like that pass you by. There is always a way to work your message into what they are looking for. Be the expert. Be the go-to person. Be the servant.

After you've done an interview, you definitely want to follow up with the producers, host of the show and anybody you worked with. Show your appreciation! Thank them for the opportunity for being able to work with them. Following up with a hand written note is a nice touch. Whatever you can do to show your gratitude will help you to stand out. This is an important piece so use your imagination.

Be quick to respond. They may need something from you (such as follow up material) and you want to make sure you are very timely and on top of responding to their needs. It's not good to have people waiting around for you.

Also, see what you can do to help promote them and the show. Let it be known to your list (online followers) and anybody you come in contact with what a great experience you had by working with that particular show. What goes around comes around, so send out as many good vibrations and compliments as you possibly can!

The core message of this chapter is **Be the Servant.** If there is only one thing that you get out of this book (and I certainly hope you get much more) is the understanding of your purpose as a human being on this planet. When you seek to serve, genuinely serve from your authentic self, then you make yourself valuable to others. In turn, you are serving yourself and creating a world where you matter.

Give what you have to offer in a way that helps other people do better in their lives. Find out what people need and give it to them, bigger and better than they would expect. How can you do this? What can you do in this moment to think of ways to serve? Who is better because of what you do today? How might you maximize, serve and celebrate this day? How might you be of service?

Notes

What do you have to offer? How might you be of service?

Notes

Summary

M

Do you feel you have more tools in your arsenal? Are you clear on what you have to offer? Are you feeling free to live your dream? I certainly hope so. It is my dream to serve you so that you can reach out and touch more lives. Anything you desire is possible, even probable, especially if you follow the principles outlined in this book.

After watching the 2013 movie, *The Butler,* about people dealing with injustices, atrocities of racial inequality, separation, killings and civil rights issues that held them back from being able to thrive in society, it became clear to me that we don't have the magnitude of those challenges to deal with today. There is no reason for you to not be fully expressing your gifts or fully putting yourself out there to serve in the biggest way possible. There is no excuse. None. It is your duty to let yourself be known. It is your duty to push yourself and make use of the talents that God has given you in order to accomplish your purpose.

Seek opportunities. They exist all around you, in any given time or place. If you don't see the opportunity - then BE the opportunity. Get in proximity with where you are most likely to align yourself with others who are of like mind with you. Approach anything and everything you do with the intent to serve.

Carry with you the power of the **5 STEPS TO WIN**. Think and be aware of other people's reality. Be open and honest. Don't wait to make things happen. Keep moving forward, one step at a time. And for goodness sake, celebrate.

You may be thinking that you are too busy, and rightfully so. You should be doing what you do best. Your time and energy is valuable and best spent solely focused on your talent, craft or skill that you have to add to the world. But don't confuse not having enough time with not having enough discipline.

Being a *Publicity Magnet* is going to help you do what you do best in a larger way so that you can make more of an impact on those you seek to serve. That doesn't mean you have to be the one taking all the steps to do things like building out your media kit, or sending information to the stations. You will grow faster and more effectively when you leverage the tools around you. Having an organization like *Publicity Magnet* at your disposal will give you the tools, resources and power needed to free you up and make better use of your time.

There are definitely ways for you to accelerate the process. Get into a mastermind group with people who are in the TV, Radio & Print arenas. This gives you the opportunity to find mentors and start working with strategic partners like those whom I have the pleasure to work with.

Publicity Magnet puts on seminars where you can network with people in the media industry. You will hear from experts who can give you the information you need. We share information and connect leaders like you with life changing opportunities.

Our program is for you if:

- You are an entrepreneur, leader or coach who seeks to improve the lives of others and get your message out through the media via TV, Radio & Print.

- You want to network with the media and experts who will help you to accelerate forward.

- You desire to team up with high level mentors.

- You want to learn how to effectively approach the media.

- You want to create powerful catchy and memorable hooks.

- You want to build your story so that you mesmerize others.

- You want to be masterfully relevant to TV & Radio shows and their audiences.

- You want to become irresistibly camera-ready.

- You want to be known as one of the elite best-of-the-best Publicity Magnets.

- You want to BE SEEN, BE HEARD and BE REMEMBERED.

If the above speaks to you, then speak to us. You have it in you to become a *Publicity Magnet* and we are committed to your success.

To arrange for a complimentary, 20-minute 1:1 coaching strategy session, feel free to send me an email at Ask@HavilahMalone.com.

If you enjoyed this information, you might be interested to know that I deliver topics like this to audiences nationwide.

Some of my presentations include:

- Become a Publicity Magnet - Why Publicity is More Powerful the Advertising
- How to Increase Self Confidence & Deliver Effective Presentations
- Turning Passion into Profits
- The Perfect Timing Formula - Get More Done in Less Time
- The Truth About Starting Over
- Getting to YES - The Best Kept Secrets to Selling Anything
- And many more...

If you'd like more information about how to book an engagement with me for your next conference, workshop or seminar, please visit www.havilahmalone.com or email me at Ask@HavilahMalone.com.

I look forward to hearing from you and seeing you get your message out to the world!

Wishing you continued success,

— *Havilah Malone*

Acknowledgments

There are so many wonderful people who have blessed my life and influenced me for the better on my path to success.

Cynthia Malone – You are more than a mother; you are my superhero, number one supporter and biggest fan. You've provided me with such a strong foundation of faith and sense of purpose. Growing up I did not always fully understand or appreciate your guidance, but time makes all things clear. I love you from the bottom of my heart and thank God every day for a mother like you.

Michael Malone – My daddy! Thank you for always keeping an open door for my outrageous ideas and ways of thinking and never being judgmental. I love you more than words can say.

Keiana Malone – To the best sister-in-law in the world. You have been a true friend and listening ear. I value you so much.

Vicki Froiland – You have been such a great friend, whenever I needed to talk you were there with pearls of wisdom to share. You've always been like a second mother to me. Thank you.

Gerald Lee – My Uncle Gerald, if you want the truth this is the man who will give it to you fast and raw but always from a place of love. Thank you for being there for me when I needed you the most.

Ron & Renee Alee – Hurricane Katrina blew me into your lives and it has been such a blessing being a part of your family.

I want to give a special shout out to my dear friends **Jason & Emily Niemeyer, Deidra Smith, Chaquina Dudley** and **Stephanie Durant.** All of you have been there for me, thank you.

To a talented Director and Acting Coach, great mentor and friend, **Kimberly Jentzen**. You truly lead from the heart.

To my tech guru and friend, **Joe Janssen**. You are a blessing in my life.

To **Saundra Richardson** and **John Kendall**, thank you for so fiercely believing in me.

Roslyn Flot – Thank you for allowing me to express my thoughts and creativity and share that with the world through my column "Havilah's Corner" in Breakthru Media Magazine for all these years.

Russell Landry – Where there is no accountability, there is no progress. Thank you for always keeping me accountable and for your contributions to making my passion a reality.

Susan Hemme – To the best writing partner in the world! You always know exactly where I'm coming from and how to express exactly what I'm thinking. Your support and diligent work is truly appreciated. You are more than a friend. You are family.

Linell King – To the man who truly gets me. "Health is Your True Wealth." You are truly a gem and an amazing coach and friend.

Lisa Lieberman-Wang, Craig Uthank and **Martyn Anstey** – Thank you all for your invaluable insights, generous support and help in making this book the best it can be.

Jim Mury – You saw the talent and drive in me, thank you for giving me the chance to show it to the world as the National Spokesperson for Hewlett Packard on HSN, QVC, Shop @ Home TV and more. You were the catalyst to so many great things, thank you!

Special thank you to colleagues, groups and role models:

Lori Stewart, Deresharee Laracuente, Rhonda Akin, Roger Wagner, Loren Woodbury, Ann McNeill, The International Mastermind Association, Napoleon Hill Foundation, Lakefront Kenner, Airport & Grapevine Congregation of Jehovah's Witnesses and many more...

Bob Noonan – To the most amazing News Director. My days at Fox 8 WVUE will always be fondly remembered due to your outstanding leadership and caring demeanor. You are a role model that I will always hold dear. To a great team of anchors, reporters, producers, PA's and crew! Love you guys

Teresa Carter – To a wonderful mentor and friend from my days at the Times Picayune.

Loral Langemeier – For teaching me how to just say "Yes" and figure it out along the way. No nonsense courage and confidence is what you impart, thank you.

Tony Robbins & Platinum Partnership Family – To all my Brothers and Sisters on the path and Tony for helping me to unleash my greatest potential. Our Plat Family helps me every day to stay on my path. Giving yourself permission to live an amazing life and contribute to others along the way is one of the best lives you can have. Thank you for your loving support and guidance. I am a better person because I know you.

Oprah Winfrey – I look to you and see a future of unlimited possibilities. Your strength and determination are the roadmap most are afraid to travel on. You moved a nation with your love and truth. You made a believer out of me and I thank you.

I am grateful to every one of you who have followed my career and supported me along the way. Please know that you are in my heart and genuinely a part of making this happen.

And special thanks to all of you for reading this book! I know your lives are busy and I appreciate you taking the time to hear what I have to say. I don't take that lightly and am here to serve you in any way I can. *You were born to win!*

About the Author

Havilah Malone is a visionary and treasure hunter for proof of what's possible in life. Born and raised in Kenner, Louisiana, she graduated from the University of New Orleans at the age of 19 with a major in Dramatic Arts and Communication, and a minor in Psychology. As the daughter of an International flight attendant, from infancy this visionary began to travel the globe developing a passion and curiosity about the world and exploring all the great possibilities life offered.

Havilah started her career in the Fox 8 newsroom as a production assistant and eventually began field producing show segments. She has worked with the Travel Channel, AMC and many Indie projects acting, producing, directing and editing as a certified Avid editor.

Her passion for broadcast media and helping others landed her a starring role in Style Networks TV show *The Amandas*, where she helped families and businesses get organized. The multi-talented Malone has also starred in commercials, films and modeled for Sears, FashionWeek New Orleans and more.

With a keen eye for business and technology she was lead to computer giant Hewlett Packard as a District Sales Manager, managing a $100 million+ multi-state territory for nearly a decade. During her tenure with HP she had the distinct privilege of serving as the National Spokesperson on **QVC, Home Shopping Network, Shop at Home TV** and more. Her charisma, dazzling smile and business savvy lead to millions of dollars in on-air sales and a raving fan base.

With her intimate knowledge of the media world and keen understanding of the needs of business owners Havilah founded *PUBLICITY MAGNET*, a firm of consultants, business strategist and media experts dedicated to helping entrepreneurs, coaches, authors and leaders grow their business and get their message out to the world via FREE Publicity on TV, Radio & Print.

Havilah is a regular contributor to BreakThru Media Magazine. Her column *Havilah's Corner* covers a range of empowering and hard-hitting topics, life advice, and business tips as well as spotlighting people making a difference. She also serves as a Radio Show Host and Spokesperson for **The International Mastermind Association**, a non-profit organization focused on helping people build wealth in all areas of life using the *mastermind principle* based on concepts in Napoleon Hill's "Think and Grow Rich". She is also in development of a TV show.

Havilah is a dynamic speaker and youth advocate. She

passionately encourages people to follow their dreams because she believes anything is possible. **Her nurturing spirit, inspirational voice and magnetizing personality are not only a unique representation of the city she calls home but also the future of the country.**

To arrange for a complimentary, 20-minute 1:1 coaching strategy session or to get more information about how to book an engagement with Havilah Malone for your next conference, workshop or seminar, please visit www.havilahmalone.com or send email to Ask@HavilahMalone.com.

Made in the USA
Columbia, SC
12 August 2018